Original title:
Ferns on the Bookshelf

Copyright © 2025 Creative Arts Management OÜ
All rights reserved.

Author: Henry Beaumont
ISBN HARDBACK: 978-1-80581-879-3
ISBN PAPERBACK: 978-1-80581-406-1
ISBN EBOOK: 978-1-80581-879-3

Whispers of Green Beneath Dusty Tomes

Among the volumes piled high,
A leafy friend peeks slyly by.
With tales of mulch and sunlit beams,
It giggles softly while we dream.

When knowledge blooms in a petal's dance,
The margins fill with leafy prance.
A sneaky sprout with stories new,
Who knew it'd steal the show from you?

Tendrils of Thought in Sheltered Nooks

In cozy corners where books reside,
Little tendrils peek, with green to bide.
Whispering secrets from every page,
As if they're scribes, writing sage.

With giggles trapped in dusty text,
They giggle at our prose perplexed.
A leafy muse with roots in dreams,
Who knew they'd launch our thoughts like beams?

Lush Secrets Amongst the Pages

Between the chapters thick and grand,
Lush secrets weave from hand to hand.
A leafy laugh escapes each book,
Come closer now, take a good look.

With every flip of a papered line,
They nod and whisper, oh so fine.
Unraveled tales of ancient lore,
Bright spirals sprout from the floor.

Verdant Companions of Forgotten Stories

In the narrative of dusty dreams,
Verdant companions stick like schemes.
Their humor blooms through every tale,
As they plot a green escape to sail.

They tickle tales with leafy cheer,
While pushing dusty books far near.
In hidden plots, they find their place,
Bringing laughter to the reading space.

The Silent Guardians of Written Worlds

In twilight corners, they stand tall,
With spiky arms that seem to call.
They watch the pages turn and flip,
As stories dance in literary grip.

Dust bunnies hide from leafy eyes,
While characters plot their sweet reprise.
"Shh!" they whisper, in verdant cheer,
As plots unfold, they laugh and leer.

Bookmarked by Nature's Patina

Between the tomes, they wiggle and sway,
Guarding secrets with leafy play.
They laugh at scholars, so rigid and stern,
While underneath, the stories churn.

Tales of dragons, sorcery grand,
Foliage tickles the books by hand.
With each new tale, they shimmy and shake,
Ensuring no page is left opaque.

Memories Woven with Celestial Green

Old tales shiver in the dim-lit room,
While green fingers stretch to dispel the gloom.
They giggle quietly when owners forget,
The plots that twist, the laughs unmet.

In the margins, whispers curl and dip,
As vines plot mischief with leafy tip.
Characters blush in tales of old,
As laughter echoes, their antics bold.

The Language of Leaves and Lore

In leafy tongues, they spin and twirl,
Mimicking laughter in a leafy whirl.
Each story's ink blends with their hue,
Creating a plot that feels brand new.

They tease the volumes with gentle tease,
Tickling tales with a rustling breeze.
So many chapters stretched upon the shelf,
They wink and nudge, like playful elves.

Lush Leaves Among the Pages

In the corner they lie, quirky and grand,
Planting secrets in tomes with a leafy hand.
They sway to the rhythm of stories untold,
Chasing dust bunnies with a heart made of gold.

Each time I pull one, it gives me a wink,
"Stop reading that drama; just give me a drink!"
They drink up the plots that they surely despise,
While I laugh at their frowns and their rolled-up green eyes.

Silent Guardians of Literature

Guardians they are, with a twist of delight,
Standing watch over novels, day and night.
With a rustle of leaves, they whisper and tease,
"These plots are too dry; let's liven with ease!"

When I ask for advice on the latest romance,
They giggle and sway, giving books quite a chance.
"Just add a few spores, let the foibles unfold,
And sprinkle some laughter with stories retold!"

Nature's Ink on Whispered Tales

Ink never drips from their delicate stalks,
Yet they scrawl their own tales in mysterious talks.
Each page that they touch turns a vibrant shade,
As characters bloom in their soft, leafy glade.

They play hide and seek with the dust on the shelves,
Turning history's poets to cheeky green elves.
"Join the fun," they say, "you've read it for long,
Add a dash of green wit, and you can't go wrong!"

Verdant Echoes in a Wooden Nook

In a snug little nook where the sunlight's a friend,
Green bundles of giggles erupt and extend.
Their laughter erupts like a sunny bouquet,
While pages are turning in their floral ballet.

"Tell us your tales, oh brave literature,
We'll add our own spice, of that we're sure!"
And as plots get twisted and narratives spin,
Those leafy companions always wear a grin.

Guardians of Knowledge in Botanical Form

In dusty tomes where stories lie,
Little green sentinels peek shy.
Guarding wisdom with a smile,
Waving leaves that think in style.

Whispers of pages turn in night,
While leafy friends join in delight.
Who knew plants could be so wise?
With stories spun from roots that rise?

Tangled Thoughts of Green Heroines

In pots of clay where dreams may sprout,
Adventures weave and twirl about.
Green heroines with leafy flair,
Swapping secrets without a care.

They giggle softly, sharing tales,
Of secret worlds where logic fails.
Chasing shadows, peeking bright,
In every book, they feel the light.

Spheres of Comfort in Tangled Roots

Roots intertwine like thoughts in knots,
Building worlds in novel plots.
These quirky greens seek cozy nooks,
Nestled snug between the books.

With every turn, they sway and dance,
In leafy skirts, they take a chance.
Whispering dreams to tales profound,
In each soft leaf, joy's found.

A Lush Canopy of Written Wanderlust

Under leafy canopies so wide,
Adventures grow without a guide.
Words are leaves that sway and flop,
In this garden, stories hop.

Each plot a vine that climbs so high,
Reaching out to touch the sky.
With winks and nods, they weave delight,
In written paths, we find our flight.

The Imagination's Lush Retreat

In corners green they sit and stare,
Whispering tales beyond compare.
With leafy laughs and twists of fate,
They judge my choice of books, oh great!

I swear they giggle, just out of sight,
As I reach for stories late at night.
Between the pages, they dance and sway,
Critiquing my taste in a leafy play.

Their fingers soft on spine and cover,
I swear they'd make a clever lover.
With quips and quotes like casual foes,
They always know the best prose flows.

So let them linger, full of charm,
Adding mischief, adding calm.
In this nook where laughter thrives,
I'll keep them close for fun-filled lives.

Ferny Embrace of Forgotten Texts

Amongst the dust, they stand so proud,
Whispers of gossip through the crowd.
A novel's joke, a poetry plight,
They roll their leaves at my bookish plight.

Oh, how they bask in olden tales,
As I flip through with weary gales.
With every sigh, they shake and tease,
Prompting me to drink and sneeze.

These leafy friends, so wise and spry,
Conjure giggles as I pass by.
They boast of plots I've yet to read,
In their embrace, I feel no heed.

So here they thrive, those sprightly greens,
In laughter shared, the humor beams.
With every glance, they shake their head,
At all the books I've left for dead.

Literary Flora: Chronicles in Green

With pages crinkled, worn, and dog-eared,
The stories beckon if you've steered.
"Pick me!" they squeak, "Let's have some fun!"
While leafy buddies bask in the sun.

Oh those tendrils, with eyes so bright,
Rolling their greens in pure delight.
As my mind wanders, they twist and curl,
In this odd literary swirl.

They gossip as I ponder each page,
With leafy laughter, all the rage.
They shout, "Ditch the rules, dive in deep!"
Inviting whimsy as I leap.

Through crowded shelves, they spread such cheer,
Turning the whispers into loud roars here.
In this leafy realm of books and lore,
Life's just a joke we all adore.

Tales of Old in Ferny Embrace

Gather 'round, o' leaves of green,
Here's a tale that's rarely seen.
In stories old and bindings weak,
They smile at every word I speak.

With each chapter, they sway and lean,
Catching giggles, quite unseen.
As I stumble on plot twists galore,
Their whispering chuckles leave me wanting more.

"More tea!" they cry, "For this old tome,
Let's make this couch our leafy home!"
Beyond the spines, in bright expanses,
They throw a party — oh, how it prances!

So let my books gather dust and lore,
With green companions, who need no score.
In laughter shared and tales embraced,
I find my joy, so firmly placed.

Spirals of Life on Stacked Stories

In the corner sits a plant,
Whispering tales both grand and scant.
Around its fronds the dust does cling,
As if it knows the joys of spring.

With fingers crossed and eyes all wide,
It keeps our secrets safe inside.
Oh, the stories that it's seen,
In the jungle of my library scene.

Grows with glee in the afternoon sun,
Outshining all, oh what fun!
It laughs when I forget to water,
A silent prankster, ever a trotter.

So here's to leaves so green and sly,
A witness to the laughter nigh.
In this cozy cluttered nest,
Life's spirals swirl at their very best.

Resilient Growth Among Bound Tomes

Lurking between the spine and page,
Is a green one full of leafy sage.
With every book, a new disguise,
Growing wise while I theorize.

Often I hear it giggle light,
When I fear I've lost my sight.
Pointing to dusty tales in rows,
Its leafy gestures surely knows.

How many hours have I spent,
Chasing thoughts—oh what a rent!
While rooted there, it mocks my plight,
In the chatter of the late night light.

Yet still it thrives, through thick and thin,
Jokes on me while I search within.
Resilient, crafty, and full of jest,
Amid the tomes, it knows me best.

Fern Fronds and Forgotten Lore

In the nooks where shadows play,
A leafy sprout holds court each day.
With tales of yore and giggles low,
It entertains those in the know.

Each frond a banner of ancient cheer,
While peeking at books like it's the beer.
It's the gossip of a thousand lines,
In its little world where mischief shines.

We share our coffee, I'll admit,
As literature turns and gets a split.
Each sip a tale, a cosmic thread,
Yet it rolls its eyes at what I said.

Amid the papers, ink, and dust,
That cheeky plant remains a must.
A keeper of secrets and marvelous lore,
Its charm ensures I'll read once more.

An Oasis of Leaves and Lore

In a world of tomes and crinkled texts,
Lives a leafy friend who often vexes.
With a twist and turn, it starts to sway,
Mocking my thoughts, making play.

At times it trips on piles of tales,
Rustles loudly, and flails itsails.
"Do you even read?" it seems to tease,
While I stumble on, begging for ease.

Pages flutter, and dust bunnies dance,
In this oasis where ferns take a chance.
Who knew wisdom had such a face?
With every curl, it claims the space.

So here's to the laughter, the roots intertwined,
A world of leaves and laughter aligned.
In the garden of knowledge, a comical sight,
Where nature giggles through the night.

Literary Botanica: A Green Reverie

In corner nooks where stories bloom,
Leaves whisper secrets, dispel the gloom.
A tale unravels, much like a vine,
With every chuckle, the roots entwine.

Books stacked high, all green and bright,
They plot and conspire, a leafy delight.
Oh, the plot twists are quite absurd,
As plants read prose, and giggles are heard.

Each page a petal in joyful sprout,
They jest and jive, amid the shout.
With ink that drips like dew on leaves,
The laughter echoes, the heart believes.

From spine to spine, the stories play,
As fronds reach out to steal the day.
With every turn, a whimsy grows,
In this green world, hilarity flows.

Wandering Roots of Narrative Adventures

In this cluttered realm where fiction spills,
Roots stretch deep, as curiosity thrills.
Chasing shadows in dust motes' dance,
Each leaf's a hero, take a chance!

Characters tumble like clumsy ferns,
Stumbling through tales, in whimsical turns.
With laughter sprouting, tales take flight,
As green companions join in the light.

A quirk in the binding, a laugh with a leaf,
Their stories blend, a comic relief.
Like vines that embrace, snug and tight,
In their leafy laughter, we find delight.

Oh, how they chatter, roots intertwine,
Every adventure, a punchline divine.
In this quirky grove of snickers and glee,
The narrative wanders, forever free.

A Shelf of Syllables and Serendipity

Upon the shelf, where tales collide,
Foliage giggles, cannot hide.
Words are budding, sprouting in cheer,
As playful thoughts blossom near.

The plot thickens like moss on stone,
With each twist, a chuckle is grown.
In leafy realms where stories weave,
Every page a trick up the sleeve!

Imagine a fern with a wink, not shy,
It teases the reader, 'Oh my, oh my!'
As ink flows like sap, in comical streams,
Turning our daily thoughts into dreams.

With every verse, a dance of green,
Narratives frolic, never mean.
In the bookish jungle, we spin and sway,
Syllables giggle, leading the way.

Lush Landscapes of Ink and Imagination

In fantasy fields where stories grow,
Each leaf a character, stealing the show.
With a quirk of nature, they twist and tease,
Turning plots into laughter, with the greatest of ease.

The pages rustle like a gentle breeze,
And crinkle like laughter—oh, what a tease!
With every chapter, a new tale unfurls,
Frolicking fables in a world of swirls.

Green thoughts sprout up, like ideas anew,
Each curly frond, a giggle, it's true!
From roots of nonsense to leaves of mirth,
In this lush landscape, humor finds birth.

So come take a stroll, in this verdant parade,
Ink-filled laughter never will fade.
In gardens of whimsy, where stories bloom,
The ink and imagination always consume.

Poetry in the Presence of Greenery

In a world of pages, plants do peek,
Whispering secrets that make me squeak.
With every giggle from the leafy bunch,
I fear they're planning a playful lunch.

Books lean in closer, what do they hear?
A shushing forest that loves when I'm near.
With rhymes and roots, they dance in delight,
The ink grows green under soft moonlight.

As I read aloud, they sway in glee,
Are they critiquing my poetry?
"I'll write you a sonnet," I jokingly say,
"Just promise not to steal my words away!"

So here I sit, the paper and leaves,
In a partnership full of giggles and grieves.
For in this bookish, leafy chaos,
Who knew that plants could be so pious?

Shelves Beneath a Ferny Fringed Sky

Upon my shelves, the greens reside,
With every book, they sneak inside.
"They're plotting," I chuckle, "to grow a verse!"
"Does this one rhyme? Or just sound worse?"

The novels whisper, "Water us right!"
As if I'm their keeper both day and night.
With each turn of the page, they puff with pride,
Stealing focus, they dance and slide.

"Oh dear books, your spines look so stiff,
Let this greenery give you a lift!"
With sprightly feathery fronds, they cheer,
As I sit and giggle, it's clear they're dear.

In the laughter of leaves, who needs a muse?
Their frolicsome spirit, I surely won't lose.
So here on my shelf, amidst tales that shine,
I find folly in nature, a blend so divine.

Nature's Bookmark in a Bookish World

In this realm of stories, green marks the way,
Imposing plants have come out to play.
"Mark my page!" they cry, just like a knight,
Who knew that a leaf could make such a sight?

A tale goes on, characters are bold,
Yet it's the fronds that quietly scold.
"Did you notice us lounging with charm?"
While I stifle laughter, they mean no harm.

In my chapters, they weave their own plot,
A twist in the tale that I'd surely forgot.
"Doing yoga with prose is quite chic,"
They thrum with laughter, "It's nature's technique!"

So as I turn pages and read through the night,
My leafy companions bask in the light.
For in this realm, the words often bloom,
With humor and greenery lighting the room.

Sprouts and Sentences Intertwined

Little sprouts giggle as I compose,
Peeking from stories that no one knows.
With leafy laughter tickling my mind,
I pen down the joy of this friendship entwined.

Between chapters and laughter, the fun never quits,
As greens do their jig while my pen softly flits.
"Did you catch that pun?" they gleefully tease,
I nod in agreement, they sure aim to please.

In this tangled web of words and of fronds,
They mimic my writing with whimsical bonds.
"Let's sprout some ideas that truly inspire,"
Leaves leap and twirl, setting thoughts on fire!

So let's toast to the pages in all of their cheer,
With sprouts by my side, I have nothing to fear.
For every sentence, there's laughter to find,
In this bookish jungle, with greens intertwined.

Lattice of Leaves and Literary Spirals

In a world where pages rustle and sway,
Green whispers dance in a quirky ballet.
The words sometimes giggle, the commas they prance,
While stories unfold in a leafy romance.

Books wear their green hats, a flamboyant attire,
As characters plot, conspire and conspire.
A plot twist that tickles, a subplot that's spry,
In this green literary world, let's soar and fly!

From shy violets reading in evening's soft glow,
To daisies debating the best way to grow,
The pages are filled with a chlorophyll hue,
In a garden of tales, there's always something new.

Words leaf through the chapters, amusingly bold,
With puns that are sprouting like stories retold.
So join the green laughter, come take a look,
In this whimsical web of a whimsical book!

Stories Breathed Amidst Herbal Hues

Between the pages, where laughter is bred,
A tumble of stories, a garden of dread.
The herbs hold the secrets, they giggle and peek,
While narratives blossom, cheeky and sleek.

Chapters like basil, fresh and divine,
Add spice to the tales, a hint of good wine.
Cilantro takes notes as the thyme gives a wink,
While sentences simmer, at the edge of the sink.

Each pun's like a pinch of that salt from the shore,
In the potpourri plots that we yearn to explore.
The laughter of laughter, a sizzle of fun,
In this herbal escapade, the joy's never done.

So come take a whiff of these stories anew,
Where the words are as green as the morning dew.
In this meadow of text, let your spirits arise,
With whims that take flight, to the writer's surprise!

The Verdant Guardians of Literary Realms

In a realm where the written and green intertwine,
Sit the leafy guards on their throne made of pine.
They chuckle at plots that twist and turn tight,
Casting shadows on words as day surrenders to night.

With their leafy crowns, they give witty advice,
On how to write tales that are rare and precise.
'Write bold!' they dictate, their voices like chimes,
As the pages erupt with rib-tickling rhymes.

The daisies dive into novels with flair,
While sunflowers recite like they just don't care.
Each chapter a dance, each line a small jest,
In this jungle of humor, there's never a rest!

So raise your ink pens and take up the task,
Let the guardians guide you; behind leaves, they bask.
With laughter they nod, as the stories take flight,
In the glorious glow of green literary light.

Tales with a Green Thumb

With a twist and a turn, the stories all sprout,
In a funny old library, where giggles clout.
The tales take root, in this playful parade,
Where mischief and magic comically invade.

In pots filled with wisdom, ink spills like rain,
As chunks of absurdity tumble and strain.
The characters prance in their leafy attire,
Throwing shade with a chuckle, lighting literary fire.

There's a plot involving daisies who plan,
To write their own novel as part of the plan.
With a dash of humor and a sprinkle of zest,
These blossoms of laughter are truly the best.

So plant all your phrases, let them grow tall,
With a green thumb of laughter, you'll have it all.
In the garden of stories, vivid dreams are spun,
Where laughter takes root — oh, what funny fun!

Page Turners and Plumed Dreamers

In a world where stories flutter,
The leaves compete with tales that stutter.
They whisper jokes from spines like books,
While readers give them curious looks.

A poet sighs, his pen distraught,
As green companions plot and squawk.
They joke about their leafy fame,
While he just scribbles, feeling lame.

But as the pages turn, they sway,
With every word, they dance and play.
A symphony of laughter grows,
Among their branches, wisdom flows.

So turn the page, and take a chance,
Let botany and books entrance.
For in this leafy, funny space,
We find both joy and green embrace.

A Shelf of Secrets and Soft Fronds

Hidden truths on wooden shelves,
With soft fronds whispering to themselves.
Books stand tall, adorned with green,
A quirky view, a funny scene.

Between the rows of tales and lore,
A secret life you can't ignore.
The flora giggles, leaves the clue,
While silly authors break the queue.

A novel ponders 'What is next?'
While plant puns keep the suspense vexed.
The irony is rich and lush,
As every spine begins to hush.

So dare to look among the stacks,
Where nature blends with quirky facts.
In every laugh and joke you find,
The stories bloom, and hearts unwind.

Green Dreams in Literary Lanes

In alleys where the tales unfold,
Live creeping vines both shy and bold.
They share their dreams with writers lost,
In leafy laughter, not a cost.

The words float up like dandelion,
While plants conspire, never bowing.
A pun is tossed, a leafy snicker,
Oh, how the plots can thicken quicker!

Each spine aligned like soldiers neat,
With soft fronds tapping tiny feet.
The stories leap, the laughter spins,
As green begins where the tale begins.

So wander through this vibrant maze,
Where greenery and stories blaze.
In every turn, a chuckle waits,
In leafy lanes where laughter's fates.

The Bibliophile's Secret Garden

In the garden of forgotten reads,
Blossoms sprout in quirky beads.
Tales entwined in playful glee,
As pages hum a melody.

The roots, they twist and turn about,
While curious thoughts begin to spout.
A bookworm's grin as green leaves play,
In this sanctuary where they stay.

With every chapter, laughter grows,
As bugs tell tales that no one knows.
The blossoms bloom with quirky prose,
Reminding us how fun it goes.

So enter now this leafy nook,
Where joy and stories dance on hook.
In every giggle, charm will stay,
In the garden where we laugh and play.

Ephemeral Growth on Knowledge's Edge

In the sunlit corner, leaves take a stand,
Whispering secrets only they understand.
Pages may wrinkle, but green is quite bold,
Searching for sunlight, a story unfolds.

Dust bunnies laugh, as they dance in the air,
Books stack up high, but they don't seem to care.
Roots stretch for wisdom, but warmth's not a crime,
Jokes on the readers, they're wasting their time!

With ink-stained fingers, we turn every page,
Finding our fortunes within every age.
Yet beneath the spine, a comical sight,
Plants playing peek-a-boo, in morning light.

Knowledge is thorny, but plants sure take breath,
Mirth seems to flourish, even midst death.
For laughter is growth, and it thrives with a cheer,
So bookworms and greenery, let's give a beer!

Pages and Petals: A Quiet Accord

Petals and papers, a curious team,
Each with their stories, wrapped up in a dream.
Authors provide words, but leaves spill the tea,
Sharing old tales of a grand bumblebee.

A spider spins webs over chapters anew,
While readers sip coffee, 'tis quite the view.
Dew drops act like bookmarks, for tales yet untold,
As laughter erupts, and the moments unfold.

Words and green foliage, a quirky alliance,
Swaying together in mild defiance.
So as chapters crack open, the leaves start to wave,
Reminding us all, that the world's ours to save.

For humor, it nests, where the sunlight does stream,
With petals of wisdom, we twirl like a dream.
Through pages and plants, the universe paves,
A haven for giggles, where chaos behaves.

Humble Bloom in the Realm of Words

In a land of soft pages, a shy bloom appears,
Wiggling its petals, dispelling our fears.
Despite all the scribbles that clutter the map,
It holds onto laughter, just like a good chap.

This little green critter, called Hector the Leaf,
Serves humor and wisdom, a double belief.
With roots sunk in stories and stems made of jest,
The joy of its presence, one can't quite contest.

As bookworms gather, their laughter takes flight,
Over tales of adventure, and creatures of fright.
Yet beyond every chapter, secretly grown,
This humble hero finds warmth all alone.

So let's crack a book, and let giggles arise,
In the company of green, truth wears a disguise.
For humor's the nectar that fills up the room,
With petals as pages, we bloom and we zoom!

Botanicals Breathing Life into Prose

In shadows of knowledge, green creatures reside,
They giggle and whisper, like squirrels they hide.
Books stacked like towers, a fortress of lore,
Where laughter's the treasure, an unspoken score.

Poking their heads through gaps between tomes,
These jesters of nature, they make themselves homes.
With every new chapter that turns like a page,
The plants crack a joke, releasing their sage.

Through humor they grow, intertwining their fate,
In the realm of the wise, they're the life of the great.
For plants and their wisdom go hand-in-hand fun,
Breathing fresh laughter like rays of the sun.

So tip your hat kindly to growth in your space,
As it adds to the wisdom, a smile on each face.
In the corners of stories, they twirl with delight,
For fun's in the air, as day turns to night.

Whimsy and Greenery Tucked Away

In a corner, greenery thrives,
With books piled high, their wisdom jives.
A squirrel once tried, with a leap so bold,
To read a tale, or so I'm told.

Pages turned in sunlight's grace,
While shadows dance, they weave a lace.
A cactus rolled its prickly gaze,
On stories spun from leafy haze.

Readers giggle, what a sight,
A fern in a hat, oh what a plight!
Whispers echo soft and bright,
As laughter blooms in pure delight.

Each tale a jest, a playful tease,
With leafy friends, it's sure to please.
In pockets of green where chuckles reign,
Let imagination burst, never mundane!

The Chronicles of a Leafy Haven

In this cozy nook, tales come alive,
Where plants and pages laugh and thrive.
A novel's plot twists like a vine,
And pen in one hand, a sprout is fine!

Oh, how a leafy friend can muse,
Picking favorites from the literary brews.
A parrot squawks, "Pick me, it's fun!"
While poking at stories, one by one.

The ferns debate which book is best,
A classic comedy—or a thrilling quest?
As I sip my tea, they chatter away,
Plotting shenanigans for the day.

With a chuckle and twist, they turn the page,
Every leaf a character, on the stage.
In this leafy haven, joy is free,
Where whimsy stories flow like tea!

Nature and Narrative: A Quiet Concord

In a whispering green, tales unfold,
Where bits of laughter scatter like gold.
An ivy climbs to steal the show,
As rhymes and stories joyfully flow.

A plot thickens like morning dew,
Spinning yarns in shades of hue.
The potted sage rolls its wise old eyes,
As antics unfold with surprise.

The novels giggle, the leaves rejoice,
In the library's corner, they find their voice.
Once a squirrel claimed a tome to munch,
That's bookworming taken to lunch!

Paginated dreams weave bright and green,
Where absurdity reigns, and joy is seen.
We chuckle here in nature's nest,
Where humor and greenery are truly blessed!

Inked Fronds and Bespoke Tales

With inked fronds upon the shelf,
Each leaf a tale, a quirky elf.
A rubber plant plots its adventures bold,
In stories where laughter is a must-told.

The cat tiptoes with dubious grace,
As novels tumble, leaving their place.
A ferocious plot stirs with mischief,
The fern laughs loud, "What a gift!"

In a world where pages flutter and dance,
Nature finds wonder, not just by chance.
A bookmark droops, a story awaits,
While friends in green giggle, "Let's celebrate!"

These tales unfold in joyous delight,
As laughter echoes, innocent and bright.
In this leafy realm, let the wonders swell,
With inked fronds here, we know all is well!

Tapestry of Text and Verdancy

On shelves they perch, leafy and spry,
Guarding the tomes with a watchful eye.
They chuckle as pages unfold with ease,
Attempting to read, with a rustle of leaves.

With chapters of green and stories to tell,
They whisper to bookworms, 'Come, read us well!'
But every time fingers brush through a page,
They shimmy and shake, setting thoughts off stage.

The novels sigh deep, feeling quite green,
As mossy mischief dances between.
'We're not mere decor,' they giggle and tease,
'We're the sidekicks here, take us with ease!'

So next time you ponder a book to explore,
Remember the greens that amplify lore.
For in this wild world where stories entwine,
The lush and the letters together combine.

Wild Words Nestled in Green Embrace

Amidst the spines that lean to one side,
A feathered quill finds a place to hide.
In a jungle of paper, with whispers around,
Lies laughter and secrets that leap with a bound.

They share all the tales of wild escapades,
As leaves gather round to provide their shades.
'You won't believe what the plot twist unveils,'
Said a raucous fern, spinning funny tales.

One by one, the books hold their breath,
As laughter and lushness escape from the depths.
'What's a plant's favorite genre?' they chime,
'Anything that roots for a sunny good time!'

So take a good look, and you just might find,
That laughter and life share a curious bind.
For amongst all the pages, in colorful clout,
The wildest of words have taken a route.

Hidden Narratives Amongst Lush Canopies.

In dappled light, tales twist and twine,
Beneath the brows of a verdant spine.
Boozy fables sprout with a flick of the breeze,
While laughter erupts from the pages with ease.

Between chapters deep, the leaves have their say,
Making moments quite sprightly, oh what a display!
Each plot a wild romp, with laughter entwined,
As words take flight in the leafy unwind.

'What has pages but never can fly?'
A leafsmith giggled, 'Oh my, oh my!'
With puns aplenty, and quips that ensue,
The tales leap like bubbles, both giggling and new.

So when you sit down with a book on your knee,
Cast a glance at the greens that sway with glee.
They're vaults of jocundity, hiding within,
A treasure of laughter, where stories begin.

Whispers of Green Beneath the Dust

Dust motes swirl like characters that play,
As greens crack jokes in their own leafy way.
Each spine on the shelf holds a punchline or two,
While shadows of stories dance, 'What's new, what's new?'

With potted potions and tales stacked high,
These leafy jesters keep spirits awry.
'What did the book say to the curious light?'
'Stop shining so bright, you're ruining my night!'

Each petal a witness to words that are sown,
They giggle together, their laughter full-blown.
'A plot twist is funny if it rattles and rolls,
Try not to get tangled in our leafy shoals!'

So next time a story takes you by surprise,
Let the greens share a chuckle, oh how they rise!
For wisdom and wit in the wild intertwine,
Through giggles and pages, a vibrant design.

The Charm of Pages

In the quiet corner, they sit so proud,
Whispering secrets, never too loud.
A dust mote party, on stories they dine,
With a sprinkle of laughter, all things align.

Jokes about roots, and puns about leaves,
They tease the tomes, oh how it grieves!
But amidst the chuckles and gentle quips,
They swell with wisdom, on paper slips.

The Dance of Leaves

Twirling and twinkling, they sway all day,
In the light of the sun, they come out to play.
A pirouette here, a shimmy there,
They dream of the forest, without a care.

Pages turn briskly, like rustling wings,
As laughter ignites with the joy that it brings.
'No need for a book, just watch us groove!'
With every soft shake, they begin to improve!

Sheltered Stories in a Canopy of Green

Under a canopy, stories reside,
In shades of emerald, they happily hide.
A giggle escapes from the words of the wise,
As they lean from their perch with mischievous eyes.

A curious tale to share with a glance,
They weave through the pages, inviting a dance.
"Caution!" they say, "We may spill the tea,
On how nature laughs in a library spree!"

A Sanctuary of Sages and Sprouts

In a nook of the library, they gather in cheer,
Sages who've seen every novel appear.
Sprouts of all colors, with wisdom to lend,
They nod at the readers, their humorous friend.

"Don't judge a book by its cover," they shout,
"When branches can tickle, and giggles sprout!"
With each clever line, and quirky charm,
They forge a safe haven, all wrapped in warm.

Nature's Touch in a World of Words

With petals of prose and stories that bloom,
They revel in laughter, dispelling the gloom.
Nature's own humor, wrapped in green hues,
Peeks from the pages, sharing old news.

"Watch out for plot twists," they quip with a grin,
"Or a thicket of tropes that pull you right in!"
In this riot of foliage, tales intertwine,
As ink spills its magic, so pure and divine.

Flora and Fiction in Unison

Among the pages, plants do play,
They peek and stretch in a leafy display.
Books whisper tales of their vibrant attire,
While green companions plot to conspire.

The novel's plot thickens, oh what a twist,
The plants start dancing, you get the gist.
They hop and swirl, tossing dust on the cover,
Just wait, I think they're forming a lover!

They snicker softly as the chapters unfold,
With every turn, a secret is told.
One leaves a note: "My spine is so sore!"
While the other yells, "I could read much more!"

Underneath the light, they take a bow,
Shaking their fronds with the sass of a cow.
Do they ponder plot lines or just catch a ray?
Who knows? They giggle and sway all day!

Tales from the Hearth of the Greenery

In a nook full of tales, where leaves conspire,
Sitting with novels, their passions expire.
They sprout witty quips as the plots unwind,
"Don't you dare check out, or you'll be maligned!"

A cactus chimes in, all prickly with pride,
"Can't you see, I'm the one who's the guide?"
The ferns roll their eyes, with glee they erupt,
"We navigate stories—just don't interrupt!"

In the hush of the room, laughter does bloom,
As stories entwine with scents that consume.
A dandelion jokes as it floats on a breeze,
"I'm only here for the gossip, if you please!"

The shelves start a riot, books wriggle and shake,
A riot of undergrowth, for goodness' sake!
"Who needs a hero when we've got this team?"
They plot their escape to a paper-filled dream!

Intimacies of Ink and Life

In corridors of knowledge, the leaves collide,
Whispering secrets, none can deride.
"You're the plot twist," one creeps out to say,
While another just nods, "More mischief today!"

Ink spills with glee as the pages conjoin,
Scribbled ideas, where roots intertwine.
"Is it the stories or are we the stars?"
Questions arise like little green jars!

Inky fingers dance, never quite still,
A support group forms on the window sill.
"To be a good story, do you need to sprout?"
"Or is there a chance we could branch out?"

Laughter ensues, a scholarly haven,
Tales that are wild, both comic and laden.
"Oh, where will we go with adventures untold?"
"Just follow the sunlight, let wonders unfold!"

The Imprint of Nature on Printed Dreams

Beneath the dust jackets, they gather and grin,
The stories of life and the mischief within.
A whispering fern gives a playful nudge,
"Careful now, don't over-indulge!"

As pages turn rapidly, their spirits ignite,
Old manuscripts once lost now shine ever bright.
"This plot needs a twist, or perhaps a slight bend,"
While another asserts, "Wait, let's not pretend!"

Their discussions grow louder, with boldness and flair,
As vines entwine novels, a peculiar affair.
"Can plants write poems, or dance in the rain?"
"Oh, surely they can! I've seen them complain!"

So gather your stories, plant friends left and right,
For laughter and tales make the evenings so bright.
In corners of rooms where the sunlight streams in,
Nature's own antics lead the fun to begin!

The Harmony of Leaves and Prose

In the corner, a plant does sway,
Books below it, in disarray.
The pages rustle, a gentle tease,
As leaves gossip 'bout the next big breeze.

A thicket of tales, where green meets ink,
Both sit quiet, neither will blink.
The sunlight beams, a soft caress,
While writers ponder, 'Oh, what a mess!'

Yet laughter erupts from this leafy friend,
It tickles the spine, where stories bend.
With every sip of the morning brew,
The plant giggles, "I've stories too!"

As novels gather dust, it stays spry,
"Just give me water, and I'll comply."
Absurdity grows, oh plant friend divine,
What a quirky life, one leaf at a time.

Growth in the Shadow of the Classics

Among the poets and prose so grand,
A squat little guy makes his stand.
"Move over, Shakespeare, I'm here to shine,
With chlorophyll dreams and roots that entwine!"

The classics chuckle at this cheeky sprout,
"I'd write your biography, no doubt!"
"Dear old tomes, just watch me grow,
I have tales, too—more than you know!"

Between the pages, whispers abound,
Of adventurous leaves not yet found.
"Hold tight to your stories," the fern then quips,
"For I'm about to eclipse all your scripts!"

So here's to the green in a paper domain,
Where humor and knowledge intermingle in vein.
A world of wonders awaits below,
As laughter springs forth in a leafy show.

The Verdant Veil of Written Whispers

Upon a shelf, the green is sly,
Eavesdropping on the words that fly.
"Catch me a rhyme or two, let's play,
I'll leaf through your lines in a quirky way!"

With tangles of humor, it twirls about,
In shadows of authors, it cannot pout.
"Oh, what a scene of literary grace,
As I sprout up high in this crowded space!"

Everybody reads, while I get the giggles,
With every word, my little leaf jiggles.
"Doesn't it tickle, to think of the lore?
One day I'll write, just wait for that score!"

Through sapling and spines, I softly seep,
In the quiet hours, while others sleep.
A humorous garden of bobbles and prose,
Where laughter and wisdom happily grows.

A Canopy of Words and Wild Things

Under the tomes, a jungle thrives,
With tales of daring adventurer's lives.
"I'll share your secrets, don't look so alarmed,
In the canopy's magic, we both stay charmed!"

A paperback rustles, "Are you a spy?
Are you eavesdropping on the why?"
"If I were, I'd write my own book," it declared,
"Of paper and green—fear not, I'm prepared!"

So stacked up high, the laughter rolls,
As stories weave with the small, leafy goals.
Holding court in the midst of prose,
With playful gossip that ebbs and flows.

Between wild things and parchment dreams,
An odd little friendship, or so it seems.
In the chapter of plants, humor finds way,
In a world of words, let's dance and play!

Pages and Petals in Delicate Harmony

On the shelf they gather round,
Leaves and tales are tightly wound.
A story breathed in every sigh,
Between the covers, whispers fly.

Curled in corners, creeping sprout,
What's the book? Let's figure out!
A daring tale of leaf and spine,
Competing for the sun to shine.

A plot that thickens, wild and green,
The bookworm's grin is quite the scene.
Pages rustle, leaves will sway,
Who reads the book? The plants will play!

And with a chuckle loud and bold,
Each story's worth its weight in gold.
As pots and pages share a laugh,
Together they craft the perfect path.

The Wisdom of Wood and Whimsy

A tome so thick, it holds its breath,
While leafy thoughts dance close to death.
"Who turned that page?" they slyly ask,
The bookshelf shelves a leafy flask.

Old tales grow dusty, seeds of thought,
All sorts of wisdom cleverly sought.
Each chapter flaunts a cheeky glance,
While leafy friends sway in a dance.

The woodwinds play a playful tune,
As dust motes spin beneath the moon.
'What's next?' they ponder, 'Let's find out!'
A lively shoot joins in the shout!

A punchline waits at every bend,
In stories that twist, and never end.
With every word a new delight,
The laughs go on, well into night.

Plot Twists Among Lush Tendrils

In tangled tales where stories weave,
Green fingers stretch and dare to believe.
A tale of shadows, light, and fun,
The fable wriggles, yet it's oh so pun!

With leafy verses all a-jumble,
Try not to sneeze amidst the tumble.
A plot that flips with every turn,
The jokes take root, for wisdom's yearn.

In laughter, they bridge the written world,
As whispering petals gently twirled.
The punch line pops amid the leaves,
A rollicking fun that never cleaves!

Secrets simmer beneath the spine,
With every page that's crossed with vine.
In twists so grand, and jokes galore,
They cheer for more, 'Let's find the score!'

Fern Dreams in Alphabetical Order

A for adventure, up the shelf,
B for books that read themselves.
C for curling up so tight,
Where the greenery greets the night.

D for dust in a moted dance,
E for every curious glance.
F for fables that sprout and squeeze,
Giggles erupt with leafy ease!

H for humor that flops and flips,
I for imaginations that trip.
J for jokes that leaf through time,
K for knowledge in rhyme and chime.

L for laughter that sprouts between,
With every page in the leafy scene.
M for mischief upon the shelves,
Together they dream, this crew of elves!

Nature's Comfort on the Written Word

Pages turn with gentle rustle,
Greens peering from their bustle.
Whispers of a novel's flair,
Dust motes dance in sunny air.

A plot twist hides in fronds aloof,
Chapters curl, a leafy roof.
Characters may tumble and trip,
While leaves sway with a cheeky grip.

Jokes sprout where shadows play,
Puns take root, then drift away.
Books and plants, a quirky mix,
Both are better with a few tricks.

In this nook, a story brews,
Fiction blooms in vibrant hues.
Laughter fills the printed space,
Nature joins, a comical embrace.

Growth Amid the Echoes of Literature

Words unfold in spiraled time,
As leafy beings dance in rhyme.
Fables hide in curled-up leaves,
Can you hear the laughter he weaves?

A novel spills on dampened ground,
In between, the roots are found.
Characters trip on their own shoes,
While cozy plants shake off the blues.

Each stanza wraps like creeping vine,
Poets scribble, sipping wine.
Nature giggles, hears the call,
Writing's wild, but isn't it all?

A comedic twist, a clever quirk,
All the while the plants just smirk.
In margins, their secrets bloom,
Where laughter fills the written room.

Secrets Among the Green Sentinels

Layers of tales wrapped in green,
Sentinels watch, always seen.
They giggle as pages unfold,
Whispering secrets, daring the bold.

A reader sneezes, hides a laugh,
In narrow spaces, plants do half.
They plot mischief when left alone,
Jokes in the soil, only they've known.

Characters squabble, twist and shout,
While leaves gossip, never doubt.
Between the lines, a passive knock,
Nature's jest tickles the clock.

A quirky sandwich of leaves and lore,
Who knew books could giggle and roar?
In this habitat of whimsy and cheer,
Every shelf holds a shiny queer.

Inspirational Leaves of Stories Untold

Leaves flutter, stories fly,
Tales of woe, a wink and sigh.
Each volume breathes with leafy grace,
Words emerge, a leafy embrace.

Puns stick like glue on the shelf,
Nature's humor hides itself.
Adventure waits in winding plots,
Among the odds and hearty knots.

Characters climb, and others fall,
Leaves giggle as they hear the call.
Whimsy reigns where books reside,
Green companions never hide.

So grab a tale, let laughter bloom,
As the leaves hum in your room.
With every page, a chuckle grows,
In this library where laughter flows.

The Poetry of Plumes and Prose

A leafy quill upon the shelf,
Whispers tales of plant and elf.
In sunlight's dance, it sways and twirls,
Writing stories for eager girls.

The pages laugh, they come alive,
As fronds perform their leafy jive.
A chuckle here, a giggle there,
Their green ballet fills the air.

Ink stains mingle with chlorophyll,
The prose will dance and never stand still.
A narrative where plants take flight,
In their green frocks, they steal the night.

Books become a jungle scene,
Where plot twists grow, lush and green.
With every turn, a laugh, a cheer,
The pages rustle, "More plants, my dear!"

Roots of Inspiration on a Sturdy Shelf

On sturdy shelves, ideas bloom,
With roots entangled, sharing room.
They giggle softly as ideas sprout,
In leafy whispers, there's no doubt.

A vine decides to rewrite fate,
While others hang, they contemplate.
The puns grow wild, they take a leap,
Sprouting one-liners, oh so deep!

The saplings jibe, "We rule this space!"
In every nook, a leafy face.
With every tomes, the laughter swells,
"Who needs the sun? We've got these spells!"

Roots of wisdom twist and twine,
Planting jokes like a glass of wine.
Each story shared becomes a show,
In the forest of knowledge, we laugh and grow.

Silhouettes of Pages and Fern Shadows

Silhouettes dance in soft sunlight,
As shadows whisper, "What a sight!"
With every curl of leaf and page,
We giggle at their leafy stage.

The story twists, the shadows tease,
A fern that sings with perfect ease.
It's bard and plant in merry cheer,
While books look on, "Oh, dear, oh dear!"

Each character has a leafy friend,
Whose spindly limbs do not offend.
In laughter blooms a tale so bright,
Where every fright ends with delight.

As stories sprout from covers tight,
The leafy tales take off in flight.
With every turn, the humor grows,
In pages where the sunlight flows.

Planting Ideas Among Written Dreams

In gardens green of literary sway,
Ideas sprout in a quirky way.
With every thought, a petal grows,
"More laughter here!" the green light shows.

Plant pots giggle, "What's our fate?"
As books respond, "Let's celebrate!"
With every quirk, there's something new,
A story laughs, and it's all true!

Seeds of humor split and fly,
Among the tomes that loom up high.
They throw confetti, made of leaves,
"Let's write of tricks that no one believes!"

Throughout the night, the ideas twine,
In quirky ways, they redefine.
As every tale takes root and grows,
Planting dreams, where laughter flows.

Shadows of Leaves on Literary Dreams

In the corner, leaves conspire,
Hiding novels, oh, so dire.
Pages rustle, laughter spills,
As they dance on sunlit hills.

Plots grow wild beneath the green,
In the shadows, mischief's seen.
Characters giggle under fronds,
While readers ponder their fond bonds.

Each leaf whispers tales untold,
As stories stretch and unfold.
Quirky plots on every shelf,
The books want to play themselves.

Oh, the stories they might weave,
In the green, we can't believe.
Laughter echoes through the room,
Nature's voice, a joyful boom.

Nature's Ink in Every Corner

Ink spots dance like curious sprites,
Nature's touch lights up the nights.
Puns and giggles in the air,
Nature's ink hangs everywhere.

A plot twist from the leafy vine,
In this library, all align.
Silly tales of herb and root,
Spilling laughter, resolute.

With every book, a story brews,
In the corners, joy ensues.
Words and leaves start to collide,
As the yawn of dawn provides.

Nature winks with every page,
Bringing forth a playful sage.
So let's write with greenish flair,
Where laughter lingers in the air.

Syllables Wrapped in Nature's Embrace

Whispers of leaves fill the night,
Syllables wrapped, oh what a sight!
Words flutter like butterflies,
Underneath those verdant skies.

Comical plots grow tall and wide,
In the green, we laugh with pride.
Characters trip on leafy trails,
As humor fills the words like sails.

Branches tease with clever tunes,
While readers hum nature's croons.
Taking flight on playful prose,
In the green their spirit flows.

In the chaos, joy is found,
Nature's magic spins around.
Every line, a funny tease,
Wrapped in green, we all feel pleased.

Green Veils over Literary Wonders

Under green veils, words appear,
Scribbled laughter floats so near.
Every shelf calls out to play,
With leafy mischief on display.

Characters peek from leafy nooks,
Trading tales with stolen looks.
Puns spring forth like playful rain,
Nature's humor is their gain.

The shelves giggle with delight,
As words frolic through the night.
Leaves and letters twirl and spin,
In this dance, a world begins.

With every turn, a chuckle comes,
In this place where laughter hums.
So grab a book, let laughter sway,
In this green lush, let's all play.

Sheltered Insights in Leafy Folds

Amid dusty tomes, the greens reside,
Whispering secrets, a leafy guide.
Pages turning with every breeze,
Bouncing stories between the leaves.

Books look puzzled, asking why,
As plants plot how to fly high.
A cookbook's recipe for a sunbeam,
And a novel's dream of a wild stream.

The ficus hides between classics,
Wishing to be in the next antics.
While ivy plans to form a league,
To take on authors with a fatigue.

Their roots entwined in prose so bold,
Incredible tales and wonders unfold.
Imagined chats between stories and leaves,
In this corner, laughter never leaves.

Nature's Pencils Sketching Tales Untold

Among the bindings, green sprouts sway,
Their chlorophyll pencils scribble away.
Writing letters in sunlight's glow,
Plotting antics we'll never know.

Monstera dreams of a novel that's wild,
With a plot twist where the house cat smiled.
The snake plant drafts a saga of stealth,
While spindly stems giggle at bookshelf wealth.

Cacti offer sharp points of view,
While orchids suggest a romantic brew.
A jungle of humor, twists, and plots,
That even dusty old spines find hot.

So, gather 'round, you bookworm pals,
While leafy scribes dance like gals.
Lessons told with a twist and a tease,
In the realms of green, there's nothing to squeeze.

A Living Library of Soft Green Whispers

In quiet corners where shadows roam,
Leaves gather whispers, seeking for home.
Each stem an opinion, each frond a joke,
Turning pages, with laughter they cloak.

Mossy mischief in the corner bound,
Where tiny tales tumble and twound.
Gossamer thoughts on a paper thin line,
Dreams of explorers who drank verdant wine.

The zany zinnia tells of a heist,
Of shiny book spines stolen by mice.
While creeping vines giggle in the back,
Pondering what humor the grand books lack.

In this library where greens converse,
Comedy flourishes, never a curse.
So come and listen, oh curious friend,
As tales entwine and greens transcend.

Scribes of Soil in Archived Echoes

Down in the earth where the quiet's profound,
Scribes of the soil gather around.
Chortling tales as they wiggle and squirm,
They craft each story with a comical charm.

With roots entwined, they conspire to share,
A saga of sunshine and stories rare.
Every worm has a plot twist in mind,
Laughter echoing through the dark intertwined.

Beneath leafy pens, wisdom blooms bright,
Each write-up a chuckle, a sprightly delight.
The deeper the roots, the funnier the lore,
Mother Nature's giggle, we can't ignore.

So revel in laughter, dear reader and friend,
Join the soil scribes, your worries suspend.
In whispers of dirt and the tickle of green,
A library lives where humor's the queen.

www.ingramcontent.com/pod-product-compliance
Lightning Source LLC
Chambersburg PA
CBHW070319120526
44590CB00017B/2737